All Aboard

City Trains

by Jenna Lee Gleisner

Bullfrog Books

Ideas for Parents and Teachers

Bullfrog Books let children practice reading informational text at the earliest reading levels. Repetition, familiar words, and photo labels support early readers.

Before Reading

- Discuss the cover photo. What does it tell them?

- Look at the picture glossary together. Read and discuss the words.

Read the Book

- "Walk" through the book and look at the photos. Let the child ask questions. Point out the photo labels.

- Read the book to the child, or have him or her read independently.

After Reading

- Prompt the child to think more. Ask: Do you live in a busy city? Have you been on a city train? Would you like to?

Bullfrog Books are published by Jump!
5357 Penn Avenue South
Minneapolis, MN 55419
www.jumplibrary.com

Library of Congress Cataloging-in-Publication Data

Names: Gleisner, Jenna Lee, author.
Title: City trains / Jenna Lee Gleisner.
Description: Minneapolis: Jump!, Inc., 2020.
Series: All aboard | Includes index.
Audience: Grades K–1.
Identifiers: LCCN 2019022730 (print)
LCCN 2019022731 (ebook)
ISBN 9781645272380 (hardcover)
ISBN 9781645272397 (ebook)
Subjects: LCSH: Street-railroads—Juvenile literature.
Subways—Juvenile literature.
Classification: LCC TF705 .G54 2020 (print)
LCC TF705 (ebook) | DDC 388.4/2—dc23
LC record available at https://lccn.loc.gov/2019022730
LC ebook record available at https://lccn.loc.gov/2019022731

Editors: Jenna Trnka and Sally Hartfiel
Designer: Molly Ballanger

Photo Credits: B&M Noskowski/iStock, cover, 6–7; alan64/iStock, 1; andersphoto/Shutterstock, 3; FangXiaNuo/iStock, 4; Craig Schuler/Shutterstock, 5; Vaternam/Shutterstock, 8–9; littlenySTOCK/Shutterstock, 9; Transport for London/Alamy, 10–11; travelview/iStock, 12–13; Jonathan Mengesha/Dreamstime, 14; f11photo/Shutterstock, 15; katatonia82/iStock, 16–17; LeoPatrizi/iStock, 18; Shutterstock, 19; Monkey Business Images/Shutterstock, 20–21 (foreground); BeyondImages/iStock, 20–21 (background); Claudio Divizia/Shutterstock, 24.

Printed in the United States of America at Corporate Graphics in North Mankato, Minnesota.

Table of Contents

Above and Below

City trains carry
many people.

They are in big cities.

Roads are crowded.
City trains help.

subway
train

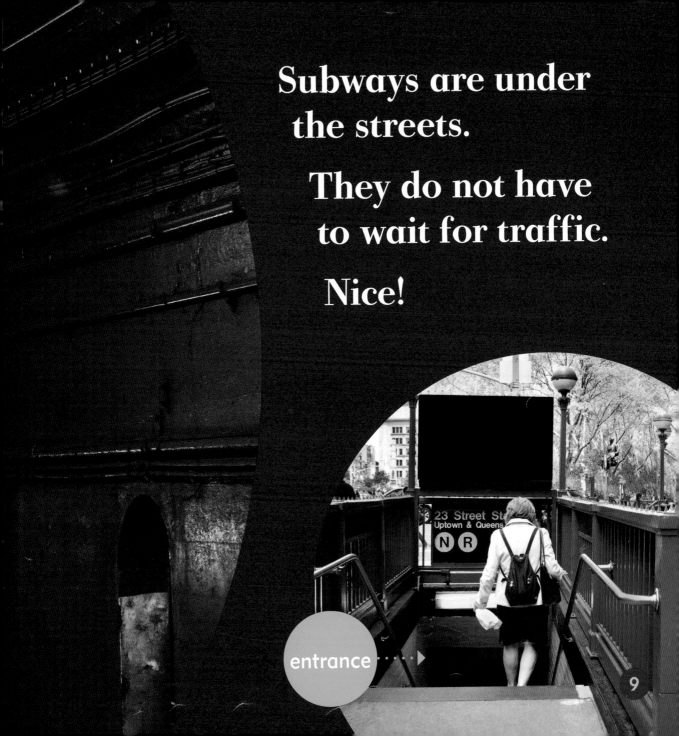

Subways are under the streets.

They do not have to wait for traffic.

Nice!

entrance ·····▶

The London Underground
is one.

We call it the Tube.

station

↑ Exit   ④⑤ Grand Central   Escalator
          ⑥ Terminal   upstairs

venue, Times Square &
Hudson Yards

← Times Square &
  34 St-Hudson Yds

Main S
Queens

42 St-Grand Cent

The New York City
Subway is busy.

It is big, too.

It has 472 stations.

Wow!

Other trains go above busy roads. This is the Chicago 'L.' Parts are elevated.

Traffic goes under.

wire

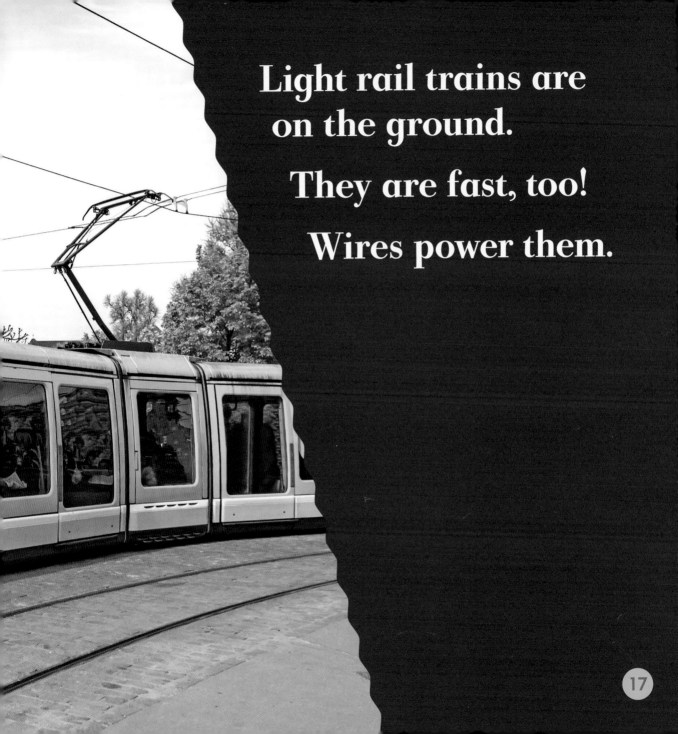

Light rail trains are on the ground.

They are fast, too!

Wires power them.

City trains have many cars.

car

People get in
and out fast.

19

Have you been on one?

New York City Subway Map

Take a look at this map. It shows where the New York City
Subway runs. All of the routes are underground.

— subway route

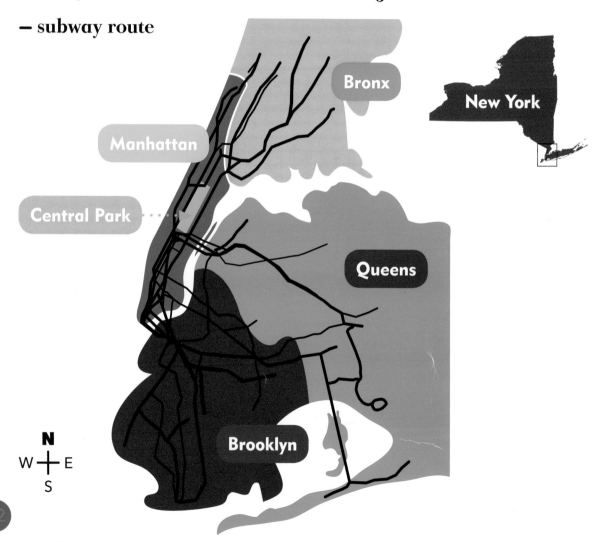

Picture Glossary

elevated
Raised.

light rail trains
Electric rail trains on street level that are powered by overhead wires.

stations
Places where train tickets are sold and passengers are let on or off.

subways
Electric trains or train systems that run underground.

traffic
All of the moving vehicles on a particular road at a particular time.

wires
Long, thin, flexible threads of metal that conduct electrical currents.

23

Index

Subway

To Learn More

FACT SURFER

Finding more information is as easy as 1, 2, 3.

❶ Go to www.factsurfer.com

❷ Enter "citytrains" into the search box.

❸ Choose your book to see a list of websites.